39
AF660646

NATIONAL SECURITY

About the Author

Sankar Sen is a distinguished member of the Indian Police Service. He was the Director of National Police Academy, Hyderabad and Director General of the National Human Rights Commission. He was awarded Police Medal for Meritorious Services and President's Medal for Distinguished Service. He has authored a number of books and his articles appear in well-known newspapers, magazines and journals in and outside the country. Presently, he is a Senior Fellow at the Institute of Social Sciences, New Delhi.

NATIONAL SECURITY
Problems and Challenges

Sankar Sen
I.P.S. (Retd.)

CONCEPT PUBLISHING COMPANY PVT. LTD.
NEW DELHI-110059

© Author

All rights reserved. No part of this work may be reproduced, stored, adapted, or transmitted in any form or by any means, electronic, mechanical, photocopying, micro-filming recording or otherwise, or translated in any language, without the prior written permission of the copyright owner and the publisher. The book is sold subject to the condition that it shall not, by way of trade or otherwise, be lent, resold, hired out, or otherwise circulated without the prior publisher's written consent in any form of binding or cover other than that in which it is published.

The views and opinions expressed in this book are author(s) own and the facts reported by him/her have been verified to the extent possible, and the publishers are not in anyway liable for the same.

ISBN: 978-93-5439-055-5

First Published 2021

Published and Printed by

Concept Since 1974

Concept Publishing Company Pvt. Ltd.
A/15-16, Commercial Block, Mohan Garden,
New Delhi-110059 (INDIA)
T: 91 11 41101460, 91 11 25351460, 91 11 25351794
E: publishing@conceptpub.com; *W*: www.conceptpub.com

Cataloging in Publication Data--Courtesy: D.K. Agencies (P) Ltd. <docinfo@dkagencies.com>

Sen, Sankar, 1936- **author.**
National security : problems and challenges / Sankar Sen.
pages cm
Includes index.
ISBN 9789354390555

1. National security—India. 2. Police—India. 3. Internal security—India. 4. Terrorism—India. I. Title.

LCC UA840.S46 2021 | DDC 355.0330954 23

Preface

The book contains a bunch of articles relating to national security published earlier in different journals and newspapers. They cover diverse issues—crime, policing, terrorism and other disruptive developments impinging on national security. Located in a violent neighbourhood, India today confronts serious threats to national security spawning from cross-border terrorism sponsored by Pakistan. There are chapters in the book on global terrorists like Hafiz Saeed, Masood Azhar, delineating how they have become liabilities for Pakistan and proving to be albatross round its neck. Hillary Clinton's aphorism that you cannot keep a serpent in the backyard and hope that it would only bite the neighbour and not you, is coming true.

Endless war in Afghanistan is dragging on but now America's decision to drawdown its troops and extricate itself from Afghan quagmire and the re-ascendance of the Taliban in Afghanistan will compound India's security concerns. There are also many other chinks in the national internal security architecture. Neglect of police reforms is making the police dysfunctional and politicized and not able to cope with growing internal threats and challenges.

I do hope that the chapters in the book will be of interest to security and law enforcement officers, academics as well as informed members of the public, and stimulate reflection over the issues concerning national security.

Contents

Section I

1

Killed in Line of Duty

Hemant Karkare was a brave, upright and no-nonsense police officer, admired and respected by all. He was, as many of his friends and colleagues have iterated, knew his job well, and did not bend before pulls and pressures coming from different quarters. During the terrorist carnage in Mumbai on 26/11, he led his men from the front and was a victim of terrorist bullets. He, along with a number of policemen died with boots on while combating a diabolical and orchestrated terrorist attack. It was, indeed, martyrdom. Hence, Sadhvi Pragya Thakur's astounding and atrocious statement that Hemant Karkare tortured and implicated her in a false case, and his violent death was due to her curse, is very unfortunate and dismaying. One fails to understand how her curse has had the potential of causing death of not only Hemant but of many more police officers, who had nothing to do with the blast cases being investigated against her. It was an insult to officers and men who shed their blood for the country.

Bharatiya Janata Party, which is supporting Pragya's candidature for the Lok Sabha elections from Bhopal, has dissociated itself from her shocking statement. She has now issued a qualified apology to the effect that she is withdrawing her statement because it may "benefit the enemies of the country". Sadhvi Pragya remained in jail for about nine years. Her allegation of torture in Malegaon bomb blast case remains unsubstantiated. National Human Rights Commission, which probed into the allegations of torture levelled by her, found that the charges were not borne out by prison, police and hospital records. The Supreme Court also had come to the same conclusion. Hence, it seems that allegations of torture levelled against Karkare and the police under him are the outcome of anger and frustration due to long incarceration, and not grounded on evidence.

The decision of the BJP to give ticket to a candidate, who is accused in a criminal case, in a very important Constituency, is open to serious objection. Of course, many candidates, belonging to different political parties, with criminal background, and also, being charge-sheeted in very serious cases, are standing for election in State Assembly and Lok Sabha. The nexus between criminal dons and political netas is a matter of deep concern. The present electoral law does not bar it. The situation has further worsened because the mafia dons have now discovered that it is smarter and better to emerge as netas, instead of standing behind them. This malaise of the body politic was highlighted by the Constitution Review Committee chaired by Justice M.N. Venkatachaliah, continues unabated. According to the National Election Watch's analysis of the affidavits of a number of candidates, in the first phase of election shows that criminal cases are pending against a good number of them. Public interest would have been better served if BJP, instead of projecting Pragya Thakur as a mascot of Hindu nationalism, and trying to appeal to the lowest common denominators, avoided giving ticket to her. This would have refurbished the image of the party and enhanced its appeal to the informed public.

In this country, another issue to be mulled over carefully is the effect of these thoughtless pronouncements on police morale. The job of the police, by its very nature, is unbelievably thankless. One astute police scholar, Ben Whiteaker, has said, "Janus-like, we have turned two faces towards the policemen. We resent him when he enforces law in our case, yet demand his dismissal when he does not elsewhere. We want crime to be eradicated, but only by the use of sporting methods." Unthinking and unmerited denunciation of the police by the public, and more so by political leaders, has an unsettling effect on the police morale. The psychologists have demonstrated that self-regard is linked with perceived regard for self by others. Therefore, frequent police bashing by members of the public, and their political masters, and incompatibility of demands on the police and thanklessness of the job, breeds cynicism in the police. They lose professional pride and dignity, and develop negative feelings against life, work and the people, in general.

Hemant Karkare was a blue-blooded Maharashtrian Brahmin. He was accused of pro-Islamic tilt and anti-Hindu bias because in Malegaon blast case he ordered charge-sheeting Pragya Thakur and her group, which included officers from the army. Karkare had to face fire and brim stone, but he did not waver. Later on, investigation of the case was taken up by National Investigation Agency. Without commenting on NIA's investigation, one can say that Karkare's investigation was on correct track, and that he was not vindictive. Karkare and his team of investigators, after painstaking investigation, unearthed the role of an ultra Hindi group—Abhinav Bharat, including Sadhvi Pragya and Lt. Col. Purohit. Both Shiv Sena and BJP, hauled Karkare over the coals and dubbed police investigation as "sinister campaign". They planned to organize a bandh, Karkare's martyrdom, during Mumbai's terror attacks, silenced the critics. Denunciation of a dead man, a victim of spite and rancour, who cannot reply to the allegations, is sad and unfortunate.

Investigation of cases against the terrorists is difficult and daunting. It requires painstaking and meticulous collection of evidence spread over different states and countries. Such investigation will be hobbled and handicapped if the investigators fear that politicians will not hesitate to run them down on communal grounds. This will be highly discouraging and demotivating.

Terror has no religion. A police officer has to be neutral in his work and conduct. There is reason to fear volley of allegations will continue to be fired by Pragya Thakur and her followers against Hemant Karkare. Police fraternity and members of the public should come forward to defend honour of a brave heart.

2

Suicide Bombings

Suicide bombing is becoming the most dreaded form of terrorist attack in many countries of the world. In the recent devastating terror strike in Pulwama (Jammu & Kashmir), a Kashmiri youth owing allegiance to the terrorist outfit Jaish-é-Mohammad (JeM) rammed a car, laden with explosives, into a CRPF convoy, killing 42 young CRPF Jawans. This was perhaps the most terrifying terrorist attack in the recent history against the Indian security forces in Jammu & Kashmir, which brought India and Pakistan to the brink of an armed conflict. Though serious breaches of the laid-down security procedures facilitated the terrorist strike, emergence of suicide bombing, as a means of terrorist strike, is darkening the security scenario in Kashmir and projecting the looming threats of similar strikes by indigenous Kashmiri militants, in future. Suicide bombing was not witnessed in the early days of terrorism in Kashmir and Punjab. The first most daring case of suicide bombing was assassination of Rajiv Gandhi by LTTE cadre in 1991. The Chief Minister of Punjab, Sardar Beant Singh was the next victim of suicide terrorism in Chandigarh in August 1995. The first suicide bombing in Kashmir took place in April, 1999, in Badami Bagh area, when a Jaish militant launched suicide attacks on Indian Army 15 Corps Headquarters.

Suicide bombing first hogged the limelight in April, 1983, when the terrorist network of Hizbullah attacked the American Embassy in Beirut, and later, in the same year, devastated US Marine headquarters in Lebanon. The success of Hizbullah suicide bombing inspired the Liberation Tigers of Tamil Eelam (LTTE) to take resort to suicide bombing in a big scale in their suicide operations. The suicide bombers constituted an elite corps and occupied a privileged position in LTTE. They were separated from ordinary cadre, and kept in isolation. Tigers are perhaps the only terrorist outfit who have been responsible for assassination of two former prime ministers—Rajiv Gandhi and Premadasa of Sri Lanka. LTTE's suicide missions were planned with minute attention to details, and precisely executed with lethal impact. The LTTE cadre, who was responsible for the assassination of Premadasa, infiltrated into his staff, and remained inactive for nearly two years, before embarking on the deadly mission.

Suicide bombing is an incredibly cost-effective method of terrorist operation. It is very difficult to detect and prevent such attacks as the perpetrators do not care for their own lives. Experts, who have studied the background and psychological profile of the suicide bombers in the Middle-east, found that most of them are young people, who are fanatical in their outlook and temperament. Family members of many of them had suffered persecution, or death, from the minions of the incumbent regime, and they seek to avenge it. Most of them had orthodox Islamic background. Recruiters of Hamas of Palestine, while recruiting potential suicide bombers, not only took into account their fanatical zeal but also clean background (with no involvement in criminal activities), to avoid detection by Israeli secret service.

In Chechnya, many of the suicide bombers were wives, or close relations of Chechen rebels who were killed in action in their decade-long war with Russia. They wanted to avenge the loss of their near and dear ones. The reasons were personal, and not religious, or political. But the ultimate in suicide bombing took place on 11th September, 2001, when a group of young terrorists, slammed the commercial jets in the World Trade Centre building, etc., in the USA, but the terrorists who took part in that attack, came from comfortable backgrounds, and were educated and not prototypes of typical suicide bombers.

Suicide bombers pose serious security hazards. It is very difficult to detect and prevent suicide bombers, who can always spring a surprise. But the task of suicide bombers can be made more difficult and burdensome, and the impact of the strike may be reduced by adopting various measures like strict access control, strengthening of verification procedures, etc. There should be constant training and drill of the security personnel deployed for the protection of VIPs and other possible targets and sensitive installations. There are instances where alertness of the security staff has prevented, or foiled lethal strikes. Regular briefing and constant simulated exercises are necessary to hone in their skills, and sharpen their responses. Along with the refinement of skills, there should be up-gradation of equipments and weaponry available to the security personnel.

Research works in the field have shown that most of the suicide bombing missions are not "lone wolf" operations. They are meticulously well-planned by a terrorist network. The suicide bombers are trained, motivated and radicalized before being sent on their missions. For organizing successful bombing operations, there is need for extensive underground preparation and coordination. Explosives have to be smuggled and stored properly and safely, for which reliable local support is needed.

In Pulwama case, the suicide bomber, Ahmed Dar, 20, who had gone to Pakistan in the spring of 2018, made a pre-attack video announcing his mission. It is known that suicide bombers routine make their last testament before a camera, before heading for the "tryst with destiny". In this connection, it bears emphasis that JeM's previous suicide bombers were not Kashmiris. There is now growing apprehension that Dar's example may be emulated by other radicalised youth of Kashmir. It may further give an ominous turn to terrorist violence in Kashmir and compound the problems before the security forces operating there.

Earlier, militants had to cross international borders to carry out suicide attacks. Now, local Kashmiris are volunteering for this new martyrdom. This is a very dangerous trend. Protesting youths are professing allegiance to international terrorist outfits like Al Qaeda and Islamic State. Their flags are raised in protest demonstrations, and the bodies of slain victims are wrapped in these flags. The situation is quite grim. In 2018 alone, there were 614 incidents in which 267 militants, 91 security personnel and 38 civilians were killed. Dance of death continues.

(Published in *The Tribune*)

3

Misdirected War Against Criminals in U.P.

The police in Uttar Pradesh have launched a vigorous crackdown on criminals after the Chief Minister of U.P. Yogi Adityanath has declared to make the state free of crime and criminals. Inspired by the edict of the Chief Minister, the police chief of the state has directed his officers and men to go hammer and tongs after the criminals. The upshot is that some criminals have been killed in encounters and many, out of fear of being gunned down, have surrendered. According to date, sourced from police Headquarters, as many as 1,142 encounters were recorded between March 2017 and January this year, and 38 alleged criminals were killed. Eight were killed in the last five days. Encounter specialists in the police are calling the shots. Encounters took place in Lucknow, Saharanpur, Gorakhpur, Bagpat and other areas of the state. Many criminals, out of fear, are surrendering, and many have given undertaking to the police that they would not indulge in crimes, any further.

Though the Chief Minister has given a green signal and assured support to the police, these developments are worrying and should not make one oblivious of the hard fact that police encounters are counter-productive and have many deleterious consequences. It is true that there is tacit public approval behind police encounters. Members of the public welcome the encounters as they feel that criminals must get their just deserts. The wheels of criminal justice move at a snail's pace. Trials drag on interminably. Notorious criminals get away scot- free and cock a snook at the justice delivery system. The fact of the matter is that encounters are not the problem, but symptoms of the collapsing system of justice and public demand for quick solutions to the law and order problems.

For proper and efficient functioning of the police, illegal encounters have to be firmly discouraged and not encouraged by the police leaders and professionals. They generate lawlessness within the police and breed contempt for law. To break law in the name of law enforcement has no place in a democratic society governed by the rule of law. It is objectionable because it is arbitrary as a process, and random in its effects. It is aptly said that a democratic order maintained by repression and criminality is ultimate disorder because it creates a link between social order and atrocities. The National Police Commission, in its report (Fifth Report) has perceptively observed that fake encounters have to be discouraged by the police leaders as this is not the remedy for the situation. Answer is to strengthen law and the legal process.

There is a wrong public perception that all police encounters are fake and stage-managed. There are genuine encounters when the police and security personnel attacked by the criminals exercise their right of private defence. Such encounters are justified within the framework of law with reference to Sections 97, 100 and 103 of IPC, which deal with the right of private defence of life and property. Section 46(3) of CrPC empowers police to use force to the extent of causing death to a person accused of an offence punishable with death or imprisonment for life, if such a person evades arrest, or seeks to escape arrest. Thus, legal provision exists for use of force against the terrorists and criminals that may result in their death. Thus encounters, *per se*, are not illegal.

The National Human Rights Commission, on receiving complaints of false police encounters from Andhra Pradesh Civil Liberties Committee (APCLC), regarding false encounters staged by Andhra police, it held public hearings in Hyderabad and recorded evidence. The Chairman of NHRC, in a letter to the Chief Ministers, advised them to issue directions to all the police stations on the procedures that should be followed with regard to cases where death had been caused in encounters with the police. The Commission felt that the right of private defence should not be manipulated to justify fake encounters, and the procedures of Section 46(3) of the Criminal Procedure Code should not be subverted to such an end. The procedure outlined by NHRC lays down that in the case of a encounter in which the police are involved, immediate steps should be taken to investigate the facts and circumstances leading to death, and ascertain how the offence was committed and by whom. If police officers belonging to the same police station are members of the encounter party, it will be appropriate that other police agencies, preferably the state CID, should take over investigation of such cases. Unfortunately, these salutary instruction of the NHRC remain just paper instruction, and are honoured in breach. It is not known if NHRC has taken any firm and tangible measures to ensure that its mandatory instructions are acted upon. The upshot is that tough counter-measures involving brazen violation of human rights are advocated by the police leaders and their political bosses against the criminals on the dubious ground that the latter have scant respect for human rights.

The practice of violating law, in the name of better law enforcement, is a mistaken strategy, fraught with perilous consequences. It will be arbitrary and random and will have the effect of undermining police professionalism and efficiency and encouraging lawlessness in the force. In my long years of service in the police and an innings in the NHRC, I have witnessed that, police vested with the unbridled authority to use force, become trigger-happy, and run berserk. In the name of combating crime and criminals, the police have settled old scores. Many innocent people have suffered loss of lives and limbs. Again, research study by a former DGP of Maharashtra police has unveiled how in Mumbai the police joined hands with one group of the underworld to eliminate their rivals in fake encounters.

There is another downside. Violating the rule of law will have the effect of making police scapegoats. Police officers rightly complain of inadequacies of law, and handcuffing of police by law. But they forget that when police take resort to extra-legal tactics to make up the deficiencies of law and legal procedures, they are trying to remedy the inadequacies they did not create. By resorting to illegal methods and exceeding their mandate, they not only take responsibility for crime on themselves but deflect attention to themselves for omissions of others. Again, serious violation of law, when discovered, invites outside interventions and the police officers, in trying to fend off such interventions, develop a "bunker mentality" and become less willing to be transparent. Putting it aptly, the American scholar, David Bayley, has said that "Illegality in the service of public safety makes policing a furtive and anxious activity and undermines pride which is the basis of job satisfaction."

It is reported that some retired senior police officers of U.P. have warned the police force of the risks and dangers inherent in the abuse and misuse of power. Some trigger-happy officers are likely to come to grief in due course for their over-zealousness. At that time, the political masters will not come to their rescue. They will rue like Cardinal Wolsey for their unthinking loyalty to the King, and not to the canons of law!

4

Perspectives on Police Violence

Lessons and Warnings

Cold blooded killing of a multinational executive in Lucknow by two policemen has caused a deep sense of public outrage. Police brutality has been excoriated by one and all. The police chief of Uttar Pradesh has called it a case of murder, and initiated prompt disciplinary action. The two constables, who allegedly shot dead the young multinational executive, have been arrested, dismissed from service and a special enquiry team has been set up to probe into the case. The State Chief Minister has assured all help for the rehabilitation of the victim's family. Response of the authorities has been prompt and positive. But what agitates the public mind and worries police professionals is whether incidents like these are aberrations and handiwork of a few bad apples, or inherent in the prevailing police system itself.

Some time back, when, for firmly dealing with crime and dreaded criminals, and restoring peace in the lawless state, the Chief Minister of U.P. gave carte blanche to the police to eliminate criminals through encounters, many senior police professionals including the present writer, expressed concern and pointed out that how far encounter killings will be a panacea for crime reduction, is doubtful; but the unfettered authority to the police is likely to be abused. Many innocent people will suffer. The turn of events justifies the apprehensions.

Policing, by any account, is a very complex job. The mandate of the police to use violence to curb and prevent violence makes it incumbent on the police not to indulge in unnecessary or excessive use of force. In a democratic system, there are laws and procedures to ensure that police function within the limits of law, and do not imperil lives and liberties of the citizens. But the problem arises when there is sharp escalation of crime and violence, and there is pressure on the police from the public, as well as the powers—that be, to deliver quick results by stringent counter measures, without caring for the means. Endemic delay in the justice delivery system prompts the police to take law in their own hands. The truth of the matter is, that encounters are symptoms of a collapsing system of criminal justice and shrill public demand for quick and extra-legal action. But the hard fact that cannot be lost sight of is that encounters are counter-productive and encourage contempt of law within the police. It is objectionable because it is arbitrary as a process and random in effect. Any drift of this kind is to be discouraged by the police leaders and the political masters. But if the latter encourage and endorse this trend, results can be frightening. A culture of impunity and trigger-happiness will grow, and the need for care and caution in the use of force, a hallmark of good policing, will be given a go-by!

It is reported in the press that the killer cop, Prasant Chowdhury, was known for his aggressive bearing. He was called "Chhota Don" by his colleagues. In every police force, there are some violence-prone police officers, who repeatedly figure in cases of abuse and misuse of force. In the USA, the Christopher Commission, which looked into the misuse of force by the police after the Rodney King incident in Los Angeles, could pinpoint a few officers frequently involved in blatant misuse of force. There should be no hesitation on the part of police leaders to discipline, and if necessary, to weed out these black sheep. If the police want citizens to know that police brutality is aberrant, they must isolate and discipline the trigger-happy police officers. Unfortunately, there is supervisory cowardice, compounded by systemic arrogance, which generates a belief among many police officers that they have the right to use their power and influence to punish anyone posing, according to their perceptions, threats to public order and safety. Again, in Indian police, peer group supervision is unfortunately missing. Peer supervision can be a powerful tool for ensuring police accountability and good policing. In Japan, policemen work in pairs, and there is understanding that one police man is responsible for ensuring the correct work and conduct of the other. In India, though policemen work in groups, but there is no assumption of mutual responsibility. Very often, policemen working together, fail to exercise any restraining impact on one another. At times, they join hands in the commission of illegalities.

Some columnists, as well as retired DGs of police, have attributed this reprehensible police misconduct to poor training and faulty recruitment. There have been serious and proved allegations of corruption and malpractices in the recruitment of constables in U.P. in the past. Irregularities in the police recruitment, included waving of police verifications to recruit people with criminal records, forging examination papers, fudging scores and changing laid down procedures and criteria for selection of the candidates. Training facilities in Constables' training schools, not only in U.P. but in most of the states, are woefully inadequate. They hardly receive any worthwhile human rights sensitization training. I know that in many states training schedule is regularly disrupted because of their deployment in elections and other miscellaneous duties.

Research on the use of deadly force has shown that the strict administrative control has a restraining effect. Already, there are rules and regulations in the police manuals, laying down rules for the deadly use of force. What is needed is effective enforcement of these rules. But training, though an important input, will be of no avail unless the principles and values imparted during training are strengthened and sustained by organizational culture. And here lies the rub. The culture of respect for human rights is yet to take roots in police organizations. Research studies have shown that the roots of police deviance are deep-seated. It results from ambiguous legislation, occupational culture and pressures to produce quick results. Officers' personality features represent only one element of the problem. In police forces in India, as well as in many other countries, officers are evaluated regarding the performance of their duties by the number of arrests made, cases detected and charge-sheets submitted. They are appreciated for hard-nosed policing and not for displaying concern for members of the public. A change of the organizational culture and switch over to efficient and human policing is needed. There is need to build a climate of opinion in the organization that frowns upon unnecessary display of authority and excessive use of violence by the police. Mere sanctions against some errant officers and men, for using violence inappropriately, will not help.

5

Has Indian Police Service Outlived Its Utility?

Indian Police Service today is facing almost an existential crisis. There is constant denunciation of Indian Police Service officers by members of the public, media and political parties. Failures of police leaders are trumpeted, and successes go unheralded. Indian Police Service is one of the three All India services of the Government of India. It replaced Indian Imperial Police (IP) in 1948, a year after India got Independence. Members of the service are selected after a tough All India service examination conducted by UPSC, and later on go to occupy leadership positions in the state police and central police forces.

During the British rule, members of the Indian Civil Service (ICS) and Imperial Police (IP) were viewed with distrust, bordering on revulsion by the political leaders of the country. They were berated as collaborators of the foreign masters. Many senior political leaders, after Independence, were of the view that senior services have outlived their utility, and should be scrapped. Fortunately, independent India's first Home Minister, Sardar Patel, was a visionary and a man of practical wisdom. He understood that to hold the country, just after attaining Independence, together and keep at bay the forces of disintegration and chaos, there was need for well-trained, efficient and effective civil and police service. If senior officers could work for the foreign powers effectively and efficiently, there is no reason as to why they should not serve the country with same earnestness. Even before Independence, he persuaded All India Congress Party to agree to the continuation of two All India services, and declared that the "Union will go if you do not have an All India service, insulated from pulls and pressures, and with independence, to speak out its mind." This he wanted to secure by the recruitment through UPSC and through Article 311 of the Constitution.

The present strength of the Indian Police Service is around five thousand. The members of the service are bright, alert and qualified young men and women. Though the minimum qualification is a graduation degree, many of the entrants are far more qualified and more accomplished. During the last two decades, many doctors, engineers and management graduates have joined the service, and added to the talent pool. David Bayley, an internationally renowned police scholar, was highly impressed by the calibre and competence of IPS officers, and said in his book *Police and Political Development in India* that "to talk to an IPS officer is to talk to an educated man and political development in India. .... I do not believe that an American school graduate, or a college graduate will show up as well."

Initially, women were loath to join the Indian Police Service in view of the prevailing notion that the service is meant for tough muscular men, and women will not be able to cope with the rigorous requirements of the police job. The myth was exploded by Kiran Bedi, the first woman to join the Indian Police Service. She was like a battering ram. She broke the walls of the male fortress, and inspired in the coming years many young women to join the Indian Police, and rendering valiant service to the country. Many of them have outshone their male counterparts in their commitment and for the police leaders, first few years after Independence were relatively smooth and trouble-free.

Problems and challenges affecting law enforcement and good governance soon surfaced in the country. This happened largely due to the decline in the quality and probity of the political leaders, and their lack of vision. During the early years of Independence, political masters at the helm were educated, committed and sensitive, with respect for rules and norms. Brazen interference in the matter of transfer and postings of officers was not the rule but exception. I had the opportunity to work with Chief Ministers, who would show respect to senior officers and listen to their views before issuing any peremptory orders. They were not guided by narrow partisan considerations. But with the passage of time, political masters began to assert themselves, and there was increasingly brazen political interference in police work. Police leaders also abjectly capitulated and carried out the dictates, at times illegal and irregular, of the political masters. This transformed the police into defenders of the establishment, and not upholders of the rights of the people. The spirit of service to the people, particularly the poor and the marginalized, no longer animates them. As a result today, police have become alienated from the public, and function as the police of the ruling party, and not the people's police. Upright officers, with spine, are marginalized and asked to cool their heels in inconsequential postings, with little work to do. Politicization has snapped the chain of command and control, corroded discipline, and made the police leaders beholden to the politicians of the ruling party.

Allegations of corruption are also darkening the image of the service and showing it in a poor light. When I joined the service, number of dishonest officers, both in IAS and IPS cadre, was few; they were known and frowned upon. There is now a sea change in the situation. Charges of corruption are coming thick and fast against many IPS officers, including young officers with three to four years of service. For insulating the police from extraneous pressures, and implementing the core recommendations of the National Police Commission, the Supreme Court issued a number of directions in Prakash Singh's case. Ten years have rolled by, but almost all the states, through various strategies and subterfuges, have evaded implementation of the apex court directions. The Supreme Court has also not cracked the whip.

There is also another unsettling development adding to its irrelevancy of Indian police service. Political leaders in the states, for obvious reasons, feel more at home with state police cadre officers, and are not in favour of posting of IPS officers in their States. This is a dim, short-sighted and opportunistic view.

Notwithstanding criticisms and controversies, the fact cannot be gainsaid that bright, well educated and qualified Indian Police Officers, with wider vision and horizon, have added value to the service and raised its level. They have also functioned as unifying links and acted as bridges between state police and central police forces. In a bewilderingly diverse country like India, with many faultlines, their role in law enforcement has been of cardinal importance. Many IPS officers have won public encomium and admiration for their outstanding performance of duties in difficult and challenging circumstances. Many have ushered in innovative changes in police work. IPS officers coming back from deputation to the Centre carry back with them rich and varied rich experience, which invigorate police administration in the states. But unfortunately, way things are drifting, do not augur well for future. Unless some meaningful steps are taken to reverse the trend and importance of the service is acknowledged, there is a distinct likelihood that the Indian police service, unappreciated by the political masters, and unloved by the public, will outlive its utility and relevance, and slide into oblivion.

6

CBI in Turmoil

The ongoing developments in the Central Bureau of Investigation are unfortunate and deplorable. The Director and the Additional Director of the Bureau are locked in a bitter feud which has virtually split the organization. The apex court has now intervened and is enquiring into the unsavoury charges and counter-charges. This indeed is perhaps the darkest hour of the organization. It is facing severe flakes from different quarters. However, there are strong reasons to hope that the Bureau will be able to weather the storm and regain its lost honour. This is because in the Bureau at different levels there are a large number of officers of probity and professional competence, who have done outstanding investigation in many difficult and complicated cases and won laurels for the organization. Thorough investigation of the CBI in Rajiv Gandhi murder case, Bombay bomb blast case, and many other complicated cases has been acclaimed by all. In many controversial and sensational cases occurring in different parts of the country, there is public demand to entrust the investigation to the CBI. It has not forfeited public trust.

The Central Bureau of Investigation was set up under the Delhi Police Establishment Act (DPEA) in 1946. During the early years, the organization, under able and upright Directors like D.P. Kohli, F. Arul enjoyed enviable reputation for transparency and technical competence. It selected officers carefully and brooked no interference in its work. For IPS officers, deputation to the CBI was a prestigious assignment, as they could function free from the pulls and pressures of the state politicians.

Decline of the CBI and its politicization started during the emergency. Shah Commission, which enquired into the excesses perpetrated during the emergency, perceptively observed that in the final analysis "the fairness and objectivity, with which an organization functions, would depend on the extent to which the higher executives of the organization are allowed to function freely and objectively, and, at the same time, ensuring their accountability to statutorily constituted bodies." Over the years, successive governments at the centre, through pulls and pressures, tried to ensure that the CBI, in politically sensitive cases, toes the line desired by the government. Autonomy of the CBI, as one of its Directors frankly conceded, became a myth, and the organization was subjected to constant external pulls and pressures. In the words of the eminent jurist, Fali S. Nariman, the CBI has been functioning "not by notes on the files but on nods and winks of the Ministers, or senior officers in-charge of administrative ministries."

In the Coal Block allocation case, the Supreme Court had to rap the CBI for showing the status report to the Law Minister and officials of the coal Ministry, for making deletions and additions, which virtually changed the heart of the status report, and subverted the integrity of the investigation. It dubbed CBI as a "caged parrot" which has to be liberated. Unfortunately, that goal has remained unrealized. Section 4 of the Delhi Police Establishment Act provides that the CBI will function under the "superintendency" of the Central Government. In the case of Vineet Narain (better known as Hawala case) the Apex Court observed that Section 4 of the

Act cannot be construed so as to prevent actual supervision of an offence by the CBI, and the Central Government is precluded from issuing any direction to curtail its jurisdiction to investigate into the offences. In the Hawala case, the apex court adopted the doctrine of "continuing mandamus" that allowed it to issue interim orders from time to time. The apex court gave the power of superintendence over the CBI to the Central Vigilance Commissioner (CVC), but it was only with regard to cases registered under the Prevention of Corruption Act. Thus, control of the CVC over the CBI is partial and shared. Recording of the ACRs is with the government, and the superintendence of the CBI in all other cases, is with the government.

Now the selection of the CBI chief is done in accordance with a new procedure prescribed in Lokpal Act, 2013. He is appointed on the recommendation of a committee comprising the Prime Minister, Leader of the Opposition in the Lok Sabha and the Chief Justice of India, or a judge of the Supreme Court nominated by him. The present CBI chief Alok Verma was appointed by such a Committee. Verma has now approached the apex court with the plea that he can be shifted only by the select Committee and not by the CVC, who has no authority to do so. The issue awaits Supreme Court's decision. But what the CBI is now witnessing is an open and no-holds-barred wrangle between the two seniormost officers. This is shocking and disgraceful. Both Verma and Asthana did not conduct themselves with becoming propriety and grace. Promotion of Asthana as Additional Director by overriding the objections of the Director by the CVC was a wrong step that weakened the control of the Director, and created rival factions in the Bureau—a recipe for mismanagement of sensitive cases now being handled by it. Similarly, raiding the office of a DSP of the organization, and arresting him in his office, was unwarranted and avoidable. Things could have been done more tactfully and adroitly.

The Chief Vigilance Commissioner has not covered himself with glory, and seems to have acted in a manner desired by the government. His enquiry against Verma will be supervised by a former judge of the Supreme Court. The present Director in-charge Nageswara Rao took over charge at midnight, and forthwith issued orders posting out officers, who are investigating cases against Asthana. This exercise has been described by some sections of the media as "a midnight coup".

It is hoped that judicial intervention will help to set things right in the CBI. But a few important corrective measures are immediately called for. A powerful body like the CBI must have an act laying down comprehensively its duties and functions. It is missing at present. The Second Administrative Reforms Commission strongly recommended a new Act to govern the working of the CBI. The law enacted by the Parliament should seek to insulate it from extraneous pressures, and make it apolitical and independent. For this, there are models in other countries which can be suitably adopted. There have been suggestions that the CBI Director should be given an independent constitutional status, like the CAG, and his report should be laid before the Parliament. Another alternative is keeping CBI under Parliamentary control. The Parliament, through a committee, should oversee the functioning of the CBI on the pattern of the Australian model. CBI should be made accountable and answerable to the Committee. In the interest of good and clean governance, the credibility of the CBI has to be restored, and it has to be reinvigorated to make it an effective instrument for fighting the monster of corruption.

It is possible to build up a powerful and effective anti-corruption agency if there is strong political will. Nearer home, in Hong Kong, the Independent Commission against Corruption (ICAC) has done a splendid job in combating corruption and helping Hong Kong to break out of the corruption trap. The Government of Hong Kong displayed its commitment by appointing a person of unimpeachable integrity as the Chairman.

A few in-house reforms are also necessary. At present, CBI officers are mainly police officers on deputation from the states. The Bureau has to widen its horizon, and in order to be effective, it should have its own cadre of well-trained and competent officers. Recruitment of CBI officers in the rank of Dy. Superintendents of Police has been stopped for some time. This may be restarted. In CBI cadre, there should be officers on deputation not only from the police but from departments like Customs, Income Tax, and other services. It is hoped that the Supreme Court's directions will help the resurrection of the CBI.

(Published in *The Tribune*)

7

Armed Forces Special Powers Act Needs Another Hard Look

In its election manifesto the Congress, among other things, has promised review of the controversy-surcharged Armed Forces Special Powers Act. The BJP, in its turn, has said that any such move will take away the shield from the army and weaken the architecture of national security. it bears recall that during previous UPA regime, the then Prime Minister Manmohan Singh promised to consider amendments of the Act with a view to making it more humane. But this could not be effectuated because of strong reservations from the army. The Armed Forces Special Powers Act (AFSPA) was passed in 1958 to counter the growing insurgency in the North-east, and later on, was extended to the state of Jammu & Kashmir.

Indeed, some of the provisions of the Act are draconian. Section 4 of the Act authorizes arrest of any person who has committed a cognizable offence, or against whom there is a reasonable suspicion that he is about to commit such an offence. It also grants special powers to the armed forces to destroy structures used as hideouts, or training camps, or a place from where attacks are likely to be launched. Further, it provides power to the armed forces to open fire, even to the extent of causing death, if propitiatory orders banning assemblage of five or more persons, or carrying of arms and weapons are in force in the prohibited area. Section 6 gives immunity to the armed forces, discharging duties under the Act, from prosecution, or other legal proceedings, except with the permission of the Central Government.

Many human rights activists and civil society groups have denounced the Act as regressive, and very often it has been abused and misused by the armed forces. And, it has facilitated extra-judicial killings, rape, torture by the personnel of the armed forces and fuelled public anger and disaffection towards the Indian state. In Mach 2012, the UN pronounced AFSPA as violative of international law. Some other UN treaty bodies have also expressed the same view."

Armed forces, on the other hand, are of the clear view that diluting the provisions of the Act will be counter-productive, and adversely affect operations of the security forces in hostile areas. Without the protection of the Act, the security forces will not be able to function effectively and proactively in the insurgency-prone areas.

The constitutionality of the Act had earlier been questioned before the apex court of the country, on the ground that it is repugnant to the rights to equality and federal structure of the Constitution. A five-member Constitution Bench of the Supreme Court in *Naga Peoples' Movement for Human Rights* Vs. *Union of India* (1998) has held that the legislation was constitutionally valid. "It was harsh in the face of it, but it was a necessity." The Apex Court further concluded that declaration under Section 3 of the Act has to be of a limited duration and subject to periodic reviews before expiry of six months, and a person arrested under Section 4(c) of the Act should immediately be handed over to the officer in-charge of the nearest police station, so that he can be produced within 24 hours before the Magistrate, after such an arrest.

There was widespread agitation and outcry against the Act following the arrest and custodial death of a woman in Manipur. Against the backdrop of the agitation, the Government of India set up a committee under Justice Jeevan Reddy, a retired Judge of the Supreme Court, to review the provisions of the Act. It was a recognition by the Union Government that the provisions of the impugned legislation needed a hard and careful look. Justice Jeevan Reddy Committee, after examining various stakeholders, came to the conclusion that the Act should be withdrawn. It recommended that it will be necessary to insert appropriate provisions in the Unlawful Activities (Prevention) Act (1957) to provide the mechanism through which the security forces can be deployed in areas, as and when necessary. The committee also recommended creation of a grievance cell in each district of the state where armed forces are deployed. This can be an independent body that will be empowered to enquire into violation of rights by the citizens. The proposed Chapter 6(a) in AFSPA should also contain dos and don'ts for the armed forces during operations, as embodied in the judgment of the apex court.

The second Administrative Commission (5th Report, June, 2007) fully endorsed the recommendations of the Justice Jeevan Reddy Committee that AFSPA should be repealed and provisions of law needed for the effective operation of the security forces can be incorporated in the Unlawful Activities (Prevention) Act (1957).

Time has now come to take a clear decision on the continuance of the Act, without further dithering. The hard fact has to be acknowledged that it is not possible to combat insurgency in the North-east, or Kashmir, without the presence of the armed forces. The truth of the matter is that the state police forces with inadequate strength and insufficient weaponry will be unable to overcome the challenges posed by the trained insurgents aided and abetted by foreign powers. At the same time, overexposure and over-deployment of the army in aid of the civil power has to be avoided. It tends to brutalize the army, and make it vulnerable to temptations and allurements. The personnel of the armed forces require clear and specific provisions for their effective functioning and operations but, at the same time, aberrant officers, responsible for violation of human rights, have to be made accountable and brought to book with a view to keeping army morale and discipline at a high pitch.

The Supreme Court has now ended the immunity of the armed forces from prosecution by laying down that they should be subjected to thorough enquiry if they have committed any serious offence. The apex court said, "It does not matter if the victim is a common person, or a militant, or a terrorist. Nor does it matter whether the aggressor was a common person, or the state. This is the requirement of democracy and the rule of law."

Numerous allegations of brazen misuse of AFSPA, and serious violations of human rights by the security forces, in many instances, have come before the NHRC. The NHRC cannot directly probe into the complaints because of the restrictions imposed by Section 19 of the Protection of Human Rights Act (PHRA). It calls for reports from the authorities of the armed forces, and makes recommendations for punishment of aberrant officers, and payment of compensation to the victims. This vicarious system of enforcing accountability does not function satisfactorily. Amendment of PHRA to allow NHRC to directly enquire into allegations against the armed forces is necessary.

Tripura, bounded on three sides by Bangladesh, has withdrawn since 2015 AFSPA, which was operational there from 2015. The state police, without the umbrella of AFSPA, have been able to combat successfully the problem of insurgency. Protection accorded to the public servants under the provisions of Criminal Procedure Code (CrPC), has been found to be sufficient. Indeed, it has been found that wherever AFSPA is operational, the army's role becomes pivotal, and the police are relegated to the backstage.

A clear decision on Armed Forces Special Powers Act brooks no delay. Experience bears out that replacement of AFSPA by Unlawful Activities (Prevention) Act will not pose problems for dealing with insurgency except in very problematic area like Jammu & Kashmir. In such states, it should be implemented only in problematic and insurgency torn areas, instead of being extended to the whole state.

(Published in *The Tribune*)

8

K.P.S. Gill: A Brief Profile

On joining Assam Police in 1965, I met Shri K.P.S. Gill quite a few times in Police functions. But first meaningful interaction with him took place in Calcutta in 1977 during conference of SSP of Naxal affected districts of Eastern States of India. We stayed together in Assam House Calcutta for a couple of days. My first impression of him was that he was knowledgeable person. His approach to policing was unconventional. He often recited Urdu and English poetry in course of conversation.

He was born on 29.12.1934 at Lahore. He was a post-graduate in English literature. He belonged to 1957 batch of IPS. He was seven-year senior to me in service and 5-year in age.

During his tenure in Assam, I had the privilege of working with him as S.P. and later DIGP Range for about six years. I came in close touch with him during these years.

On joining the Indian Police Service, Shri Gill was allotted to the Assam Cadre where, from 1958 to 1983, he handled with notable success, a range of difficult assignments including law and order management during periods of extended political strife and the emergence of terrorism in the State. His various assignments during this tenure included: Containment of mass political demonstrations and violence, Counter-terrorism, Protection of critical infrastructure, including major oil-installations and pipelines, Direction of armed police and para-military units and Law and Order Management.

Some episodes of the tenure which show Shri Gill's qualities of leadership, secular character and outstanding ability to handle difficult law and order situations are given below:

1. A Complaint of murder against the Commissioner of the Division, the DIGP range (Shri Gill), the Additional Deputy Commissioner and the S.P. Kamrup (D.N.S. Shrivastava) was filed in 1979 at a police station of the District during agitation on foreigners issue in Assam. The SHO put it up to me for direction. I went through the complaint and found that it had the ingredients of the crime. I told the SHO to register a murder case against all of us. I requested the then IGP Assam (now DGP) to consider CID investigation in the FIR. In my W.T. message to the IGP I said that I could not investigate the case as it was against me too. The case was investigated by the CID and after over three months, a final report was submitted to the court in the case as false. On coming to know this, Shri Gill was very angry with me for registration of the case. He said, "You know you have registered a murder case against me". I told him I had no alternative but to register the case. In the meantime another complaint was filed before a local Court with the same facts. We took up the matter for quashing the case in the High Court. We told the court that the case had already been investigated by the CID and found false. The Court quashed the case. Shri Gill complimented me for registration of the case at the police station as it helped in quashing the criminal proceedings by the High Court against all of us. I was

impressed with the openncss of Shri Gill for appreciating me. He also apologized for his anger earlier.

2. In 1977, a Sikh girl eloped with a Muslim student leader of a local college at Guwahati. The Sikh community was very agitated. There were stray incidents of assault on Muslims in the town. The Muslims blamed it on Shri Gill. Shri Gill told me to handle the situation. He further said that he was leaving Guwahati and will return when the situation would become normal. He was fair, considerate and did not wish anyone to doubt his integrity in such a situation.
3. He trusted his officers. Some communal clashes took place in the rural areas of Kamrup district. After informing Shri Gill I left for the place of occurrence of clashes. Shri Gill was told by the then IGP to proceed to the place to handle the situation. Shri Gill told him that it was not necessary and that I was capable of handling it. He supported his officers. All of us trusted him for his leadership.
4. Transporters had blocked the National Highway for alleged demand of money by police at the interstate check gate. In the early hours, Shri Gill was informed of it and he came to the check gate immediately. After looking at him (an officer of over 6 ft 3 inches height and if you add few more inches for his turban, he was about 7 feet), the transporters withdrew the blockade after an assurance that he would look into their complaint. He had an impressive personality.

On deputation to Government of India, he served as a senior officer in the Border Security Force in the State of Jammu & Kashmir where containment of infiltration and cross border terrorism sourced in Pakistan were crucial responsibilities.

He also served as a senior officer in the Central Industrial Security Force, with responsibilities that covered security of critical infrastructure, major industries, major ports and oil installations. Despite initial opposition from the nuclear establishment, he trained and inducted CISF cadres into the security and protection of nuclear installations in the country.

He served as Director General of the Central Reserve Police Force—a unique national armed police force that handles a range of critical internal security challenges, including terrorism, rioting and other patterns of mass political violence. He headed the Committee for the creation of a new special response Force for situations of communal violence and other patterns of mass civil violence: the Rapid Action Force (RAF).

Shri Gill led the successful campaign against fundamentalist and international cross-border terrorism in the Indian State of Punjab. As the Director General of Police, Punjab, he led a complex succession of multi-Force counter-terrorism operations that involved Armed Police, para-Military and Military units that fought and neutralized terrorism after Punjab emerged as the most serious threat to national integrity in the 1980s. He was specially inducted into the State as Inspector General of Police [Operations] and later elevated to the ranks of Additional Director General of Police, and eventually Director General of Police [DGP]. Within days of taking over as DGP, he mounted 'Operation Black Thunder', a critical success in the war against terrorism. A classical siege operation, Black Thunder was mounted against heavily armed and fortified terrorists in the holiest of Sikh shrines, the Golden Temple at Amritsar, and secured their surrender with a minimal of bloodshed. In two tenures as DGP Punjab, [May 1988–December 1990 & November 1991–December 1995], he led one of the most successful and innovative counter-terrorist operations in the history of world terrorism, bringing Punjab from the verge of disintegration to complete normalcy. This campaign was marked by radical strategic innovations and made revolutionary departures from conventional counter-terrorist theory that accorded primacy to the Army in situations of escalating terror. It was the Punjab Police that spearheaded operations in the State and in the rest of India including major metropolitan cities of Bombay, Calcutta, Pune and in the States of Uttar Pradesh, Assam, West Bengal, Maharashtra and Jammu & Kashmir. In some of these states, Punjab Police were deputed in strength for extended periods of time to assist the local authorities in putting an end to this international cross-border terrorism, that was being mounted from bases in Pakistan, and that was heavily supported by the Pakistani state.

During his Punjab tenure, he resolved two major hijacking crises involving terrorists taking control of civilian passenger aircraft and flying them into the Amritsar airport. Existing anti-hijack response procedures in the State were radically reviewed and revised under his direction to prevent the recurrence of such incidents.

After his retirement from the Indian Police Service in December 1995, he held the following positions:

He was President, Institute for Conflict Management, which he set up in 1997. He was also publisher and editor of the Institute's quarterly, *Faultlines: Writings in Conflict & Terrorism*, and publisher of the Institute's weekly newsletter, the *South Asia Intelligence Review*. As President of the Institute he advised various governments, both in India and abroad, on issues relating to counter-terrorism and internal security, and had also provided expertise on security issues to various corporate entities. The Institute had executed major projects – including the world's largest open source website on terrorism and sub-conventional warfare in South Asia, the South Asia Terrorism Portal (www.satp.org).

He was security Advisor to the Chief Minister of Gujarat between May 2002 and July 2002. He was specially appointed after major Hindu-Muslim riots and killings in the State had persisted for over two months. He brought the situation under control within a week through a major reorganization of the Police Force and para-military deployment.

He was Member of the North-East Study Group of the Ministry of Home Affairs.

He was Member of the National Security Advisory Board [NSAB] constituted by the Government of India for the period December 1998 – December 1999, to define the country's strategic perspectives and policy options on defence and internal security.

He was President, Indian Hockey Federation and Indian Hockey Confederation.

He wrote regularly for a number of journals, newspapers and magazines on politics, the economy, and governance, with a special focus on internal security and terrorism. He was also the author of *Knights of Falsehood* (1997), a book exploring both the abuse of the Sikh Identity by politicians and terrorists in Punjab, and the teachings of the Sikh Gurus.

He contributed frequently on subjects relating to terrorism and internal security, policing, politics, law and justice, to leading newspapers and magazines in India and delivered lectures at a number of premiere academic and research institutions, including the National Defence College, the National Police Academy, the Indian Institute for Public Administration and various Universities.

He was awarded Police Medal for Meritorious Services, 1972; President's Police Medal for Distinguished Service, 1982, Padamshri, 1989 and also received a large number of Honours from Public and Voluntary Organizations for restoring normalcy in Punjab after over a decade of Terrorism.

I attended his funeral at Delhi. In death also he looked not dead but live, about to speak. I saluted him and bid final good bye.

Persons of his stature are rare in police these days.

9

Lynch Killings Must Stop

Lynch killings occurring in different parts of the country are sending a grim message of dismal law enforcement and incapacity of the police to act quickly and firmly to bring the malefactors to book. It is also a fact that perpetrators of the crime in many such instances are emboldened by the acquiescence of the law enforcement authorities. After recent lynch killings in Jharkhand, Prime Minister Narendra Modi has sternly condemned the killings and castigated the offenders. He denounced mobocracy and urged the need for ensuring the safety of all citizens in a democratic order. It is hoped that his voice sanity will be heeded and stringent action taken against the killers.

Lynch killing is not a recent phenomenon. It is spiraling since last few years. According to a Reuters report, a total of 63 cow vigilante attacks occurred in India between 2010 and 2017, and in these attacks, 28 people (24 of them Muslims) were killed and 124 injured. In very few cases, offenders have been convicted. In Jharkhand itself, according to one report, 18 persons have reportedly been killed since 2016 by the lynch mob. There have been very few convictions, and here also, in majority of the cases, the victims were Muslims. Regrettably, in Jharkhand, some of the hate-mongers, who were released on bail, were honoured by some senior BJP leaders including a former Union Minister.

Lynching, or similar acts of violence take place in other societies also. In America, in the early decades of the twentieth century, there were many instances of lynching of Afro-Asians by irate white mobs who felt necessary to protect the honour of white women. American vigilantes called themselves "regulators" as they felt that they were trying to regulate the society as the situation was getting out of control.

Lynching in India is not confined to mere acts of violence by cow vigilante. Sometimes, other kinds of wild rumours anger the people and trigger mob violence against the hapless victims. In the past, a number of gory incidents had taken place, with the suspicion that the victims were child lifters. In a case in Maharashtra's Dhule district, five people were lynched by violent mob on the suspicion that they were members of a gang of child lifters. This happened because rumours were doing rounds in the area that gangs of child lifters were on the prowl. Even two policemen, who sought to save the victims, were injured. In another episode, an innocent man from Orissa was also beaten up and sustained injuries in Vadodara as he was suspected to be a child lifter. Whenever such incidents take place, a thorough probe by the criminal investigation department of the police is necessary to find out how such rumours originated, circumstances that fueled such rumours and who were responsible for spreading them and triggering mob violence. Was it a sudden unpremeditated act of violence, or planed and designed?

It is seen that members of the lynch mob are normally young poverty-stricken people, burning with anger and animated by a sense of retributive justice. They become demoniacal in their display of anger and violence. In an incident in Hapur in UP, a frenzied mob lynched a man and seriously injured his friend. A video that has surfaced shows that the injured man bleeding profusely and writhing in pain, lying on the ground, was asking for water. The cheering crowd that had gathered around him, did not offer him any water. This kind of fiendish insensitivity and sadistic pleasure is a matter of serious sociological concern. It shows deadening of the collective conscience and betokens ill for future. Similarly, a video has surfaced after the Jharkhand incident showing that the mob tied the victim Ansari to a post and beating him and urging him to shout "Jai Shri Ram".

There is also another dimension of the problem. While serving in the National Human Rights Commission, I have supervised cases where the police, with a view to getting rid of notorious criminals, incited mobs to kill them. This was short cut Machiavellian trick by the police. But because of the malfunctioning of the criminal justice system and inordinate delay in the punishment of criminals, the people also feel happy with this informal form of social control. However, this is a wrong ploy and generates contempt for law and the criminal justice system.

To contain lynch killings, false and unfounded rumours should not be allowed to circulate. Police and district administration have to ensure that they are squelched promptly. The Ministry of Electronics and Information Technology has now issued a warning to the WhatsApp over the abuse of its platform, and directed that spread of such fake messages should be contained through information technology management, and have to devise ways and means to ensure that the platform is not abused or misused by the merchants of hate and violence.

Lynch killings, in general, betoken breakdown of law enforcement. But the fact that they are mainly targeted against the Muslims, make them sinister, with diabolical repercussions. Such incidents will go to anger and alienate large sections of the Muslims, who constitute nearly one-fifth of the population of the country, and seriously retard country's progress. Last year, during the Eid celebration, some Muslim groups expressed their anger and frustration by wearing black bands. This year also, protesting against the increasing cases of mob lynching against the Muslims in the country, a large number of Muslims took out a rally under the banner of Muslims Muttahida Council (MMC). In a memorandum to the President, the protesters decried mob lynching as an organized effort to create a fear psychosis among the Muslims in the country. These are the wake up calls for the government, both at the Centre and states.

The Prime Minister has given a stirring call for not only ensuring development but winning the confidence of all sections of the community. This message has to be followed in practice, and the miscreants should not enjoy a sense of immunity. This is the acid test for good and harmonious governance. This will need resolute and robust law enforcement by the police. This will be possible and practicable if the political leadership remains firm and steadfast. The new government under Modi will have to live down the fear of majoritarianism for safeguarding the rights of all citizens, and dispel doubts and concerns of the minorities.

Section II

10

Dark Shadow of the Islamic State Over Sri Lanka

Sri Lanka experienced the most devastating terror strike on April 21—Easter Sunday. It was a bloody massacre—an attack in which more than 350 people were killed and hundreds more injured. It was spread all over the island, and perhaps the deadliest incident of international terrorism after 9/11. The targets were churches and posh hotels spread all over the island. Sri Lanka had experience of suicide bombing attacks during its war with the LTTE. But nothing of this devastating and shattering intensity had happened before. The toll would have been higher but fortunately a bomb in a posh hotel did not explode. Most of the attackers were young suicide bombers.

After any horrendous terrorist attack, there is a cry of intelligence failure. Blame is often unjustly fastened on the intelligence agencies for their failure to provide intelligence inputs that could have neutralized the attack. But this was not so in this nightmarish case. Prior actionable intelligence of the impending suicide bomb attacks was available. In early April, Indian intelligence operatives had passed on urgent information gleaned from a Tamil speaking prisoner. The names of the suspects, the targets of attacks, location of the leaders, as well as the modes of attack, including suicide bombing, were all given. But sadly and surprisingly, prompt follow up action was not taken by Sri Lankan authorities. After the attacks, the Prime Minister, Ranil Wickremesinghe admitted that he was not provided any information regarding such an impending attack. The President Maithripala Sirisena, who is incharge of armed forces as well as intelligence services, pleaded ignorance of the developments. It is unfortunate that when the island is facing a crisis of unprecedented dimension, there is lack of coordination between different agencies of the government. Indeed, it has become dysfunctional. The Prime Minister and the President are almost at loggerheads, and the communication between them has broken down. Now action has been initiated against the police chief and the Defence Secretary, but nothing can undo the catastrophe.

Sri Lankan authorities have held that the terrorist blast was a revenge for attack against the Muslims in Christchurch in New Zealand last month. This may, or may not be correct. Suspicion has fallen on two local extremist organizations—National Thawheed Jamaat and Jammiyathul Millathu Ibrahim. They are under the scanner. The Islamic State (IS), also known by the Arabic acronym Da'esh, has staked its claim for the carnage. The events highlight police lapses. It is a fact that police have not kept close surveillance over Jihadist Islamic groups in Sri Lanka. Mainstream Muslims had voiced concern about dissemination of extremist views and setting up of small Jihadi cells by suspected Islamic radicals. In December last year, following arrest of Islamist radicals, the police had unearthed a large cache of detonators and explosives in a coconut plantation, but police did not take effective steps to neutralize these radical Islamist groups. The result was disastrous. The ticking bomb exploded.

The National Security Council of Sri Lanka, presided over by the President, has become dysfunctional. The Prime Minister has not been invited for its meeting for months, and the focus of law enforcement agencies had shifted from the radical Islamic groups.

It is a fact that Islamic State, after its retreat from the Middle-east, is desperately trying to re-group and to assert. It is trying spread its tentacles in countries of South Asia. Its effort to establish a foothold in Pakistan-Afghanistan has not so far been very successful. So, it wanted to present a spectacular act of terrorism in Sri Lanka. The nature of bombing attack shows that there was long preparation and training, and very careful coordination before launching of the attack. There was intense motivation and radicalization of the perpetrators.

In its post-Caliphate phase, the IS is acting more through local proxies to assert its presence and make its influence felt. The just released video of its supreme leader, Abu Bakr Baghdadi, on April 29, delivering sermon to his followers at a mosque in Mosul, on July 5, 2014 is meant to suggest that he is alive and active. He also praised terrorist attacks by his brothers in Sri Lanka. The strategy of the IS is to organize and strengthen local groups and use them for launching spectacular attack to catch the imagination of the adherents and heighten the emotional appeal of the IS. This will enable IS to recruit more followers and strengthen its Global Mission. India is very much on the radar of the IS and we should gird up our loins and be prepared for similar terrorist strikes in days to come. Pulwama carnage in Jammu & Kashmir has shown that suicide bombing is going to become increasingly a favoured mode of terrorist attacks.

After listing of Azhar Masood as an international terrorist, Pakistani handlers will rely on indigenous recruits and not foreign terrorists.

Sri Lankan authorities have now taken extraordinary stake of banning the Riquab—a face covering worn by some Muslim women.

This is a short-sighted measure that may prove to be counter-productive. It may trigger demands for banning other identity marks for Muslim men, like beard, cap, etc. All this will have the cumulative effect of deepening the tension and antagonism between Sinhalese Buddhists and the Muslims of Sri Lanka; and sharpen the communal divide. And this what precisely the extremists want.

In the midst of all this growing tension and violence, former President Rajapaksa, who is allergic to India, is waiting in the wing to step in the centre stage. He is a popular war winning President. He feels that his moment has come. Earlier, President Sirisena and Prime Minister Wickremesinghe had joined hands to oust the authoritarian Rajapaksa at a snap election. The relation between the erstwhile friends has soured. There is growing public feeling that the island needs a strong ruler and Rajapaksa can provide the needed muscular leadership. With election around the corner, Sri Lanka may opt for a leader who, whatever his faults, can take charge of the situation.

(Published in *The Tribune*)

11

Trade War between America and China

Are They in a Thucydides Trap?

Harvard Professor Graham Wilson, in a book with an ominous title 'Destined for War—Can China and America escape the Thucydides trap?'—has emphasized the fact that two super powers—America and China—are heading towards a collusion. He raises the question if they can escape the trap of Thucydides, and find a way of moving towards some sort of "rivalry-friendship". Thucydides was the well-known ancient Greek historian, who chronicled how in ancient Greece the rising power of Athens caused misgivings and concerns in Sparta and ultimately resulted in war between the two states. This happened because incumbent power felt endangered by the emerging challenger. A similar situation, according to him, is now emerging between China and America. Steadily and imperceptibly, China has now become an economic powerhouse and a challenger to America's global supremacy in many fields. It has become the second biggest economic power after the United States, and thinks that time has come to challenge American dominance in the world.

The tariff war between the two states has gone from bad to worse. Trump has imposed a heavy import duty on a wide range of

Chinese goods. China has also retaliated with tit-for-tat measures. The present tariff war between the two countries is symptomatic of their struggle for geo-political supremacy. America wants China to open up its markets, prevent industrial espionage, stop giving hidden subsidies to State enterprises and enforce fairly and properly trade deals reached earlier. But these American demands have caused a deep sense of unease in China. China strongly feels that Western powers, particularly America, is up against China, and wants to put it down. In China now there is growing anger and revulsion against the United States. America is being viewed as a "bully and ingrate."

Initially, when the tariff war had started, many Chinese leaders and officials were of the view that the American President, a businessman, wants to cut a new trade deal with China, and USA will be satisfied with some concessions and adjustments from China. But that was not to be. America insisted on structural changes to prevent forced technology transfer to Chinese companies, copyright infringements, and hidden subsidies to the State-owned Chinese firms. China views these conditions as improper and reminiscent of "unequal treaties" which Western powers imposed on China in the past. China views it as "a century of events." The Chinese rhetoric has become increasingly combative. The State-controlled Chinese media is projecting the view that any such unequal treaty with America will be viewed by the people of China as "an act of treachery".

As the tariff war between China and America has intensified, many foreign companies are thinking of moving their manufacturing units from China and relocating them elsewhere. The on-going tariff war is hurting their competitiveness. Many American business concerns as well as foreigners are suffering the adverse fall-outs. Many American companies are reporting or projecting losses as a result of the trade war. Large US companies, like General Motors, sell more cars in China than in the United States. Some of these cars are manufactured in China. Their sales are not captured as US exports but their profits come back to Detroit. (Andrew Nathan, *Foreign Affairs*, June 27, 2019). China can also make things difficult for large US companies operating in China by toughening up quarantine and safety inspection of US inputs. It has already restricted import of rare earth materials for production of high-tech electronics in the USA.

There is a bipartisan consensus in the USA to take a tough stand against China. The previous American view that engagement with China and helping its peaceful rise will not affect American interests, is undergoing a change. There is a growing sentiment that America needs to re-balance its trade relationship with Beijing before China gets too big to compromise. But its earlier policy of accommodation is yielding place to demonization of China, and here lies the danger.

However, there are other scholars and academics holding different point of view. They are of the opinion that Beijing does not and will not imperil American hegemony. Michael Barkley, in an article in the 'Foreign Affairs', (Nov. 21, 2018), states that China militarily and strategically will not be able to overtake USA in the foreseeable future. Over-reaction to China's ascent and America's decline is unwarranted and unsubstantiated by evidence. China's power suffers from many vulnerabilities. Border defence and internal security management consume 35 per cent of China's military budget and bog down half of its action duty force. On the other hand, US military does enjoy a secure home base and focus on power projection abroad. Besides the problem of massive corruption, China has the problem of eroding workforce. According to Barkley, China and USA are not Thucydides trap because China is in no position to challenge the global hegemony of the United States.

But, unfortunately, now the tariff war between America and China is turning into a zero-sum game, with serious adverse impact on the world economy. Some well-considered sensitive steps to keep China in check are called for. But demonization of China and getting into a cold war with it will be a serious mistake. It will hurt both America and China, and also the world. The policy of engagement with China may not have succeeded in democratizing China, but it will preserve US primacy to make the world a better place.

(Published in *The Tribune*)

12

Infamous Blasphemy Laws in Pakistan

Serious agitations and mob violence rocked Pakistan over the acquittal of a Christian woman named Asia Bibi by the Supreme Court of Pakistan. She was earlier convicted under notorious blasphemy laws, which carry even death sentence. Pakistan's Penal Code prohibits blasphemy against any recognized religion. During 1980s, blasphemy laws were expanded by the military government of Gen. Zia ul-Haq. From 1967 to 2004, over 1,300 people have been charged with blasphemy. A large number of people accused of blasphemy have been murdered before the conclusion of their trials. Opponent of blasphemy laws have had to face the ire of the die-hard Islamists. Salman Taseer, former Governor of Punjab, who raised his voice against blasphemy, was shot dead by one of his bodyguards. Critics justifiably complain that Pakistan's blasphemy laws target and persecute the minorities. However, any change of laws has been resolutely opposed by the Islamic parties. On September 7, 1974, under Prime Minister Zulfikar Ali Bhutto's patronage, Ahmedi Moslems were declared as non-Moslems. It was supplemented by a new blasphemy provisions in 1986 that applied to Ahmedi Moslems.

More than ninety-six per cent of Pakistanis are Moslems. But among the countries with Moslem majority, Pakistan has the strictest blasphemy laws. Human Rights Commission of Pakistan (HRCP) has documented blasphemy cases in Pakistan. It says that Moslems constitute majority of those booked under the blasphemy laws, closely followed by Ahmedis. The laws have openly been misused to settle personal scores, and have nothing to do with religion. Mere accusation of blasphemy is enough to make someone an easy target for the hardliners. The Hanafi School of Jurisprudence, on which Pakistan claims to model the legal system, does not mandate death penalty for non-Moslems to insult the Prophet.

An attempt was made by Gen. Musharraf in his time to implement blasphemy laws in a less arbitrary manner. It was jettisoned in the face of protests from pro-Islamic parties. Musharraf was also forced to back down on a proposal in 2005 to delete the so-called "religion" column. First introduced in 1972, and later on subsequently extended by Gen. Zia, it singles out Ahmedis as non-Moslems, and requires all Pakistani passport holders to specify their religious affiliations. It erodes the constitutional and legal rights of non-Moslems and exposes them to discriminatory treatment by the state institutions.

The International Commission of Jurists has observed that Pakistan's blasphemy laws have been misused, and concerns about these draconian laws have been raised by human rights mechanisms and human rights organizations, who feel that Pakistan's offences against religions violates its obligations under international human rights laws. It has strongly asked Pakistan to review and radically amend them.

There had been furious but very predictable reactions against the judgment of the Supreme Court. Hardcore Islamists staged noisy demonstrations in Lahore and other cities, and burned vehicles, and held out dire threats to the judges who had delivered the judgment. Out of fear and panic, defence lawyers fled the country. Christian schools in Lahore were closed indefinitely for safety reasons following the protests.

Agitation was spearheaded by a party of hardcore Islamists under the banner of Tahreek-é-Labhalik, which was formed in response to the hanging of the bodyguard, who had killed the Punjab Governor. The founder of the party is a rabid venom-spewing cleric, named Muhammad Afjal Qadri.

The courageous stand of the Supreme Court judges was backed by the Prime Minister Imran Khan himself. This was remarkable because earlier, during election campaigns, Imran and his party Tehreeq-é-Insaf had proclaimed support for blasphemy laws. Displaying unexpected courage, Imran declared that the Government will crack down on the protesters, and not allow them to wantonly destroy public properties. It was given that before going for a face-off with the hardliners, the Prime Minister must have had consultation with the Army, and obtained assurance of its support. However, events have proved otherwise. As the agitation gathered momentum, the government made a U-turn and agreed to go in for a review of the decision of the court. It released the arrested agitators and put Asia Bibi on the list of people forbidden to leave the country. This happened mainly because Army is unwilling to go in for a confrontation with the agitators, who are Barelvis and supposedly more moderate than the Deobandis, from whom the Talibans draw their support. Sunni extremism in Pakistan remains mostly associated with the Wahhabis, who dominate terrorist organizations like Lashkar-e-Taiba, which was responsible for the Mumbai terror attacks, and Deobandi Sunnis, who are associated with Talibans and their various off-shoots. Barelvis are considered to be more moderate and syncretic than the Wahhabis and Deobandis because of their reverence for Sufis. Now their leader Khadim Hussain Rizvi has opted for a more violent path. Earlier, Rizvi had organized protest against changes in Pakistan's electoral laws, that changed the language of oath for the law-makers. The change in the wording of the oath was minor. It had substituted the word 'solemnly swear' with word 'affirm'. Rizvi demands a rigid adherence to blasphemy laws and stricter laws against other religious sects. He considers himself guardian of "Prophet's honour." Pakistan's military intelligence extended support to this group during Musharraf years and afterwards as a moderate alternative to the rabid Wahhabi and Deobandi groups.

It remains to be seen how Imran Khan's government stands up to the threat posed by Rizvi and his followers, who are quiet for the time being, but they will definitely try to stir up agitations if the Supreme Court in its review of the case does not reverse its judgment. It is likely that the Army would broker some sort of a truce between the government and the Islamists. The army is somewhere on the backfoot because the agitators have arraigned the Army Chief Qamar Bajwa of pro-Ahmedi leanings. There will be no change or dilution of blasphemy laws in Pakistan, and Imran Khan will have to beat a quiet retreat.

13

Importance of being Hafiz Saeed in Pakistan

Pakistan has at long last decided to initiate action against Mumbai attack mastermind Hafiz Saeed. It has prohibited collection of funds by Saeed-led Jamaat-ud-Dawa (JuD), Lashkar-e-Taiba (LeT), Fala-e-Insaniyat Foundation (FIF), as well as a number of other organizations named in the list of banned outfits by the United Nations Security Council. This decision was taken by the Securities and Exchange Commission of Pakistan (SECP)—the financial regulatory agency, under the Ministry of Finance. It warned that non-compliance with this ruling could result in heavy penalties. There are news reports that Pakistan's civilian government plans to seize control of charities and financial assets linked to Saeed. This plan of action, if implemented, will be a major move against the vast network of Saeed, which includes more than three hundred seminaries, schools, hospitals and ambulance services. According to reliable sources, JuD and FIF have more than 50,000 volunteers and hundreds of other paid workers. Hafiz even runs so Stealth Courts that decree punishment. Pakistan's reluctant move against Hafiz is in pursuance of the earlier warnings of the Financial Action Task Force (FATF)—an international body that combats money laundering and terror financing—that Pakistan faces inclusion in the watch list for failing to crackdown on financing of terrorism.

Michael Kugalman of Woodrow Wilson Centre, in his article in the *Dawn* (February 1, 2018), has said that some pressure on Pakistan may also have come from China. Though Hafiz does not pose a threat to China, Beijing fears that his ratings against India, might jeopardize China-Pakistan Economic Corridor. At present, China does not want strained relationship between India and Pakistan lest a souring of relations threatens Chinese workers and investments in Pakistan.

Hafiz Saeed carries a ten million dollars bounty on his head. He has been charged by the United States and India for links with the terrorists and masterminding the Bombay carnage, but he walks free in Pakistan, attends meetings and invited for T.V. interviews. This immunity enjoyed by Hafiz is due to some special factors and considerations. Hafiz Saeed has been looked upon as a key figure by the security establishment of Pakistan and figures prominently in army's calculations of dealing with the situation that will emerge after the US withdrawal from the region. Pakistani Generals think that sooner or later the Americans are going to leave the region. Even they might abandon the region altogether, and this might leave Pakistan alone with thousands of militants to deal with, without any international support. The army wants Hafiz to play a key role to mobilize the armed militants from different factions and either pacify their animosity towards Pakistan, or encourage the evolution as political actors.

The security establishment of Pakistan categorizes the militant groups into three spheres—first, groups that constitute threat to Pakistan only; second, groups that are threats both to Pakistan and the United States; and third, groups that are threats only to the United States and India. Hafiz Saeed falls into the third category. He is also an ideal choice for the establishment, for a number of other reasons. First, he is an anti-Indian to the bone, and patriotic in a sense that he will not take up arms against the Pakistani state. He also carries some weight with the militants, and can negotiate with them and talk to them in their language, as and when necessary.

It is known that Hafiz runs charitable and educational institutions all over the country. In the wake of 2005 earthquakes in Kashmir and 2010 floods, LeT activists won public plaudits by helping the victims in a big way. It had set up a vast religio-political training centre at Muridke near Lahore, reportedly from funds donated by Arab businessmen. It is said that JuD had transformed the area between Lahore and Gujranwala into an Islamic state.

Christian Fair, in his book *Fight to the End* refers to the 2005 manifesto of LeT—"Ham Quin Jihad Kar Rahe Hai(n)—which concedes that the Pakistan Army helps and supports LeT. The army fears that if it goes in for total confrontation with LeT, it will drive many of its cadre to enbrace Pakistani Talibans, as has happened with such outfits like Sepahi Tahiba, Lashkare Jhangvi and some sections of Jaish-i-Mohammad. Pakistan officials and generals fear a mass revolt with Lashkar-e-Taiba and Jamaat-ud-Dawa, using their extensive network to foment unrest.

Now the army wants political mainstreaming of the Jamaat-ud-Dawa (JuD). The Milli Muslim League Party, loyal to Hafiz Saeed, has been set up. Analyst Khalid Ahmed, who researched Hafiz's JuD Charity and its connections with the military, says that new political party is clearly an attempt by the generals to pursue an alternative to dismantling its militant proxies. It is clear that the army wants Lashkar-e-Taiba cadre and its leader to survive. There is also another reason—By inducting them in politics, the army wants to balance the politicians who are more and more inclined to normalize relations with India.

ISI engineered its political mainstreaming plan in April 2016. According to a former Director of the Army's Military Intelligence, the then Prime Minister, Nawaz Sharif was strongly opposed to the army's mainstreaming plan, and wanted to completely dismantle the groups like the JuD. There is also serious danger inherent in political mainstreaming of the terrorist groups. Lashkar-e-Taiba is a terrorist organization, with a record of waging Pan-Islamic campaigns. Men trained by LeT are still associated by the members of the group who have been implicated in terrorist plots in Europe, North America and Australia, though the groups leadership does not seem to have been involved. They have taken part in action within Pakistan. So it is very likely if mainstreaming of Hafiz Saeed takes place, instead of being politicized, he may make politics more religious. The civilian leadership in Pakistan is in favour of dumping Hafiz Saeed. Pakistan's Defence Minister, Khwaja Asif has said that Saeed can "pose a serious threat to the society." But the security establishment remains totally unwilling to disown Hafiz and dismantle his set-up. It remains to be seen how far it is willing to go to defy international pressure and the extent of pressure Trump administration is going to exert on Pakistan.

14

Importance of being Masood Azhar in Pakistan

China has again blocked the listing of Masood Azhar as a global terrorist by the United Nations Security Council. Over the last ten years, China has repeatedly done this. Earlier, three attempts in 2009, 2016 and 2017 were stalled by China at Pakistan's behest. China placed a technical hold, which means that the proposal will remain in deep freeze for the next six months. Thereafter, either China can lift its hold, or block it again. The present initiative of India for listing of Masood Azhar came after the vicious Pulwama terror strike, resulting in killing of forty CRPF personnel. This time, there was widespread international support of India's stand and criticism of Pakistan for providing havens to well-known terrorists. Four permanent members of the Security Council—the UK, the USA, France, Russia—and seven non-permanent members—Australia, Japan, Italy, Bangladesh, Japan, Maldives and Bhutan—joined hands in the move to designate Azhar as a global terrorist. But China did not budge and took the stand that it needs more time to study the proposal.

Masood Azhar is founder of the terrorist organization, Jaish-e-Mohammad, which is active in Pakistan-administered Azad

Kashmir. He is a native of Bahawalpur in South Punjab. He began his Jihadist career in Afghanistan's province of Khost. A devout Sunni, he went to Kashmir, and joined the ranks of Jihadists there after Soviet withdrawal from Afghanistan. He was captured and imprisoned in 1994 but was freed from Indian captivity when an Indian Airlines plane was hijacked from Nepal and diverted to Kandahar, and India was forced to release three prisoners including Masood Azhar. Another prisoner released was Omar Saeed Shaikh, who was later on convicted of kidnapping Wall Street Journalist Daniel Pearl in 2002.

There has been disappointment and frustration at China's negative and obstructionist approach. Some UN officials have clearly stated that stalled proposal can be brought before the Security Council for an open discussion. And in that event, Beijing will have to willy-nilly defend a terrorist in full public view. As a permanent member, China may veto the Resolution of the Security Council, but this will go a long way to name and shame China. France has now announced that it would freeze all the assets of Masood Azhar in their own country, and fully stand by India in its fight against terrorism. It would always stand by India in its fight against terrorism. Germany has also come forward in support of listing Azhar as an international terrorist. The European Union is also thinking on the same line. It will be a big diplomatic breakthrough for India if EU lists Masood Azhar. It will isolate Pakistan diplomatically. In a last minute bid to persuade China against blocking the proposal, the USA put out a statement saying that failure to designate Masood will go against the real goal of regional stability and peace.

Because of international pressure, Pakistan has now been compelled to take some action against the terrorist groups but these are of a cosmetic nature. Some individuals have been kept in private detention and some of the terrorist groups have been allowed to function freely, with some change of signboards and leadership structures.

Earlier, in 2016, in a statement, India had named China for blocking Azhar's listing. But this time, it has not criticized the Asian giant for halting the process. Delhi's stand is that it will not lose patience with China over Masood Azhar, and give it breathing space to resolve issues with Pakistan.

No doubt, Pakistan is China's all-weather friend. As China challenges the post cold war global order, Pakistan is likely to be its most important ally. In his well-researched book on Pakistan– 'China-Pakistan axis–Asia's New Geo-politics'–author Andrew Small has said that China wants to have Pakistan the capabilities to play the role that China wants it to play. China is also unhappy with India moving closer to the USA. This has fuelled China's suspicion that China wants to use Pakistan to keep India on tenter hooks.

Again, China has maintained links with terrorist groups like JeM, and helped them with money and small arms, to ensure that they do not target China, or support the Uyghur separatists in Xinjiang. China follows a policy of bitter repression in Xinjiang. About one million Uyghurs are imprisoned in so-called re-education (concentration) camps in Xinjiang. Pakistan remains completely quiet about it. Today, in view of growing alliance between America, Japan, Australia and India, China may try to improve its relationship with India, but it will not be done at the expense of Pakistan.

Relationship of Pakistan with the JeM is quite complex. ISI has spent vast resources to nurture it. It is an important sword arm of Pakistan in its proxy war in Kashmir. Hence, it is very doubtful if the army and the ISI will change its policy of utilizing them as strategic assets against India. Even president Musharraf has denounced the JeM, and said that Pakistan should not encourage them any longer.

However, it is to be borne in mind that listing of Masood Azhar, even if it takes place, will be symbolic. JeM is already a proscribed organization. But this has not prevented it from carrying out terrorist strikes. Things will not change unless Pakistan changes its policy of viewing the terrorist groups as strategic assets and utilizing them against India. Hafiz Saeed of LeT was listed by the 1267 Committee. Both LeT and JeM are proscribed organizations for the last twenty years. 1267 regime requests states to freeze, without delay, financial assets of the designated individuals, or organizations. But Pakistan has seen to it that their strategic assets do not suffer. Only sustained pressure from Financial Action Task Force (FATF), which has already put Pakistan on grey list, may work. But it is a matter of doubt if America will go whole hog in view of America's dependence on Pakistan in brokering peace with Talibans, so that it can pull out its troops from Afghanistan.

Masood Azhar's episode also brought to the fore the question of India's strategy and tactics of dealing with China, so long Indian policy towards China has been very defensive. India has often traversed extra miles to take note of China's core interests and respected Chinese sensitivities. But China like a big brother has not shown equal concern for India's core interests, and, at times, been uncaring. Perhaps, it is time for India to play the hard ball and not be over-deferential. India should think of options to pressure China by squeezing Chinese business interests in India, without fear of retaliation. But, at the same time, it would be improvident to reduce growing and multi-faceted relationship with China on one issue, particularly when practical gains of listing, as experience with LeT shows, are limited.

(Published in *The Tribune*)

15

Retreat of American Forces from Afghanistan

President Trump has now decided on withdrawal of the American troops from Afghanistan. His patience is wearing thin. Disagreeing with the views of some of his generals and strategic advisors, he intends to pull out of the unwinnable seventeen years old Afghan war. He had changed the earlier calculation of keeping American troops engaged in Afghanistan, without paying a too heavy political price. But if the war situation deteriorates, with the high rate of American casualties, the domestic political opinion will change. Now, situation is changing for the worse, attacks of the Taliban insurgents have become more vicious and violent, and casualties of the Afghan security forces are going up disproportionately high.

Afghanistan war has claimed more than 25,000 civilian lives since 2009. About 45,000 members of security forces have died since 2014. As a result of war and conflicts, a bountiful country has become one of the poorest in the world.

The proportion of districts under the Government control and influence have fallen from 72 per cent in 2015 to 50 per cent now. A Taliban attack on a training base for pro-government militia claimed at least forty-three lives, underlining the prevalent perilous security situation.

President Trump's decision to withdraw forces stationed in Afghanistan has evoked critical responses from many strategists and generals. A report authored for a US based think tank by James Dobbins, former President George Bush's special envoy for Afghanistan, and others, has clearly said that, in the event of a precipitous withdrawal, the government in Kabul will lose influence and legal legitimacy, and terror groups such as Al Qaeda and Islamic State would be encouraged to intensify their attacks on various US targets. Afghanistan will irreversibly slide into a wider civil war. There is also the danger that Pakistan may become more open in its backing of the Taliban insurgents.

Some US commentators have expressed the fear that Trump may withdraw the American forces even without an agreement with the Talibans because he strongly feels that important regional countries should come forward to create stable conditions in Afghanistan rather than United States, which is six thousand miles away. He has also criticized India for building libraries in Afghanistan, without providing troops on the ground. Trump's moves on Afghanistan and Syria prompted the resignation of his Pentagon Chief, Jim Mattis, who in a letter to the President wrote that the President should find a Defence Secretary who is better aligned with him.

Election of the President of Afghanistan is going to be held soon. The present micro-managing Afghan President Ashraf Ghani has not inspired confidence. There are also other candidates in the fray. A credible elected Afghanistan President will strengthen the position of the government to negotiate with the Talibans. An Afghan President, with a strong mandate, would be in a happier position to discuss issues with the Talibans.

Peace negotiations between USA and Taliban are now going along in Doha, Qatar. America is very keen to find some kind of political settlement with the Talibans. America's pointman on Afghanistan, Zalmay Khalil Zad, has expressed the hope that dialogue for a comprehensive ceasefire will be successful. The key sticking point is to persuade the Taliban insurgents to speak to the Afghan government, which they have so long derided an 'American puppet'. The Taliban will have to pledge that they would not allow international terrorist groups like Al Qaeda and ISI to use Afghanistan as launching pads for attacks against America. The US Secretary of State, Mike Pompeo has also said that the news from Doha was encouraging. America has also involved other stakeholders like Pakistan, Russia and China. Talibans have appointed Mulla Baredar Akhund as their chief negotiator. Akhund is one of the top leaders of Talibans, and is expected to negotiate on authority.

In view of Donald Trump's overeagerness to pull out American troops, and cut a deal with the Talibans, the Taliban insurgents are likely to make promises, which they have no intention to fulfil, on the assumption that America, after withdrawal, will be very reluctant to send back troops again. Hence, it is likely that the peace agreement may not offer a durable settlement but a fig leaf to cover retreat of American troops. India is one of the stakeholders in Afghanistan, but it has become marginalized in peace negotiations. Pakistan in its turn has given up the ambition of ruling Afghanistan as a puppet state, in quest for "strategic depth". It now wants an Afghan government, which is not an ally of India, and hostile to Pakistan. It realizes that without stabilization in Afghanistan, Pakistan's stability will be imperilled. Gen. Dunford, Commander of US forces in Afghanistan, was spot-on, when he said that providing sanctuary to terrorists by Pakistan will be a single biggest factor that would cause the failure of the coalition. The neighbouring power, China, wants peace and stability in Afghanistan, so that there are no unsettling repercussions on Uyghurs in the Xinjiang province of China. China and Russia are also interested in the stabilization in Afghanistan.

Developments in Afghanistan will put India in a tight spot. If Taliban strengthens its grip on Afghanistan, its influence could subsequently spread to neighbouring Pakistan and Kashmir, which would be a bad news for India. It may be quite possible that Taliban will join hands with Pakistani militants to create safe havens for terrorists targeting India.

India has made huge investments in developing soft power in Afghanistan. It is a big donor to Afghanistan, having provided about three billion dollars. The new Parliament building, Salma Dam in Herat province and a highway to Iran's Chabahar port are some of these big projects. At this stage when affairs in Afghanistan are fluid, Indian interest will require close contacts with all groups including the Talibans. But this has to be done covertly. Trump's ill-conceived Afghan policy should prompt India to reconsider its view that it enjoys the US backing in Afghanistan. It is time for New Delhi to re-assess its policy choices and engaged with the Talibans, as General Rawat has suggested, to safeguard its own interests. If Pakistan succeeds in keeping some people in the new Afghan government, who are hostile to India, it will seriously affect India's interests and assets that it has built up there over the years. India will have to thwart such designs of Pakistan.

Index